This Notebook belongs to:

NAME:______________________________

Made in the USA
Coppell, TX
05 May 2022

77441945R00066